We See You

Poems for the Unseen

Brittany Gillmore

India | USA | UK

Copyright © Brittany Gillmore
All Rights Reserved.

This book has been self-published with all reasonable efforts taken to make the material error-free by the author. No part of this book shall be used, reproduced in any manner whatsoever without written permission from the author, except in the case of brief quotations embodied in critical articles and reviews.

The Author of this book is solely responsible and liable for its content including but not limited to the views, representations, descriptions, statements, information, opinions, and references ["Content"]. The Content of this book shall not constitute or be construed or deemed to reflect the opinion or expression of the Publisher or Editor. Neither the Publisher nor Editor endorse or approve the Content of this book or guarantee the reliability, accuracy, or completeness of the Content published herein and do not make any representations or warranties of any kind, express or implied, including but not limited to the implied warranties of merchantability, fitness for a particular purpose.

The Publisher and Editor shall not be liable whatsoever...

Made with ❤ on the BookLeaf Publishing Platform
www.bookleafpub.in
www.bookleafpub.com

Dedication

For my family, my husband, my dogs, my friends,
and for everyone, really.
Every voice, moment, heartbreak, and kindness has
shaped me into who I am.
The world around me has been both my teacher and my
mirror,
and through it, I've learned to grow, to see, and to be
seen.

Preface

We See You was born from the quiet corners of life, the moments that ache, the ones that heal, and the ones that often go unnoticed. These poems are a reflection of the world around me and within me, shaped by love, loss, resilience, and the steady hum of being human.
This book is a thank you to everyone who has ever felt invisible, and a reminder that we are never truly unseen.

Acknowledgements

I am endlessly grateful to my family and friends for their unwavering love and support. To the love of my life, whose patience, laughter, and presence color every page of this book, thank you for being my anchor and my companion.

To my dogs, Conrad and Forbin, you have been my teachers, my comfort, and my inspiration. Forbin, though you are no longer here, your spirit lives in these poems, in the quiet moments, and in the love that never fades. Conrad, your loyalty and joy remind me daily of the beauty in simple presence.

And finally, to everyone who has shaped me through kindness, challenge, or example, and to those who have ever felt unseen, this book is a testament to the ways we see and are seen.

1. Our Garden

You blaze where I am soft and still,
You burn what I could conceal.
Yet in your warmth my shadows heal,
And yours find peace I feel.
The day could never bear the night,
Nor moon the mornings call.
But somewhere in our tender fight,
We learn to hold it all.
Your fire bends my trembling air,
My calm restores your flame.
We are the storm that star's repair
And love their holy name.
For greener fields may tempt the blind,
Yet truth is never new.
Each garden grows in its own kind,
And mine belongs to you.

2. The Garden I Keep

A hush of green becomes the air,
Where petals think and do not dare.
The sun a whisper through the bough,
I tend my peace I keep it now.
No visitor could find the gate,
The blossoms know they bloom and wait.
For hands that planted long ago,
To teach the soul what roots must know.
The colors blend as secrets do,
Between the gold, the rose, the blue.
What's tended thrives what's left decays,
So I return where colors fuse.

3. The Sun We Choose

The olive bends to greet the sun,
as if it knows its keeper.
Not every beam is meant for all,
Some burn, while others, sweeter.
I've learned to name the honest light,
that warms but does not wither,
and leave the rest to wander on,
their seasons lost together.
An olive branch for what has been,
a closing soft not bitter.
The heart must turn to where it grows,
and face its truest Giver.
For life is brief and suns are many,
but only one renews.
We find our peace not in the sky,
but in the sun, we choose.

4. The Sword At His Side

He stands alone on a cliff of stone,
Not really knowing where is home.
Even when climbs feel steep,
he will find himself in the hills he keeps.
The sword at his side is only for show.
Some battles are near,
and some go as far as the wind blows.
He is never truly alone,
as life swirls around him
in the rocks and the mist
Where all that lives is kissed
The peaks beyond wait,
Silent and high.
Challenge the fates,
that all mirror the sky.

5. The Girl Who Turns

She does not smile nor frown,
Her eyes a lantern site,
That spans the hush between the worlds,
for traffic made of light
The ocean wraps her temples,
The sun adores her cheek,
Her pearl a tiny oracle
of secrets beyond our reach.
She'll turn perhaps to safety,
or deeper into fear, but wisdom wears its caution,
the way her silence wears her ear.

6. Street Magic

I whisper to stop signs, make them blush,
Turn crosswalks red with a secret rush.
I spin the lamp posts; I bend the lane. CHAOS!

7. Fragments

I bite the corner of the sky,
Steal a laugh from passing time.
Walls lean in and whisper lies,
I shrug, I spit, I spit a rhyme.

8. Pulse

I kick the door, it hums my tune,
Shadows crawl beneath the moon.
Laughs combust and whispers fly,
I trace the edges of goodbye.

9. Static

I bite the wires, hum the night,
Flip the switches, spark the light.
Voices twist and tumble free,
I am the noise that bends the sea.

10. Two Fucked Up Kids

We broke every clock, ignored every rule,
Turned the world into our private school.
Blood on the sidewalks, laughter in the rain,
I want you; I fear you; I crave the pain.
We walk tightropes, strung powerlines,
Balancing the city on our reckless spines.
Your hand in mine, we wobble, we fly,
Laughing at gravity, daring the sky.
Your eyes are storms I can survive,
Your touch a map of wounds and desire.
We run reckless, untamed, alive,
Two fucked up kids playing with fire.

11. Zeus

I borrowed lightning, it hissed my name,
Chased clouds across Olympus like a flame.
Thunder rolled while I flipped the seas,
Made the mortals dance on trembling knees.
Every oath I broke, every vow I bent,
I'm the kind of God the sky can't prevent.

12. Athena

I wove wisdom into spinning threads,
Built a city out of broken heads.
Owl eyes blink at the streets I make,
Every plan I touch bends, twists, or breaks.
Knowledge is sharp, sharp as my claws,
I'm the kind of goddess who rewrites laws.

13. Hades

I chew the shadows, spit them on the floor,
Persephone dances, makes the dead adore.
The rivers shimmer, bending to her will,
I smile because our halls are never still.
She brings the spring I hold the gloom,
Together we fill every empty room.

14. Forbin

You ran too fast for time to keep,
Through sunlight, shadows, dreams and sleep.
Your bark still echoes in the hall,
A little ghost that loved us all.
The leash hangs empty, toys lie still,
Yet in my chest, I feel your will.
You stole the air, the laugh, the day,
And somehow left your warmth to stay.

15. Loyal Chaos

They bark at nothing, sprint through rain,
A furry mess, a sweet refrain.
They steal your socks, they steal your heart,
And chew the world to tiny parts.
Their eyes, bright sparks, no words can hold,
A love untamed, both fierce and bold.
They chase, they jump, they curl, they stay,
And somehow turn the night to day.

16. The Godfathers Fire

He watched the boy with eyes of flame,
A mirror bound by grief and name.
The castle whispered what was lost,
A friend, a fight, a final cost.
They called him mad, the ones who lied,
He laughed and lived half crucified.
Through veil and shadow, still he stays,
A howl that haunts the starlit maze.

17. We Are All Witches

The sidewalks shimmer under shoes,
The teacups hum their secret news.
Your shadow winks, the moon bows low,
The wind knows things you'll never show.
A sneeze can summon sparks of light,
A whisper bends the stars at night.
We're all spellbound, fierce, and free,
The world itself conspires with me.

18. Witch on the Loose

I put a curse on the traffic lights,
Made the neighbor's cat recite my rights.
I borrowed the moon,
it owes me rent,
Spilled storm clouds in the president's tent.
I stir the coffee, it screams my name,
Turn socks into snakes and never feel shame.
Every street corner trembles, every shadow sneers,
I'm the kind of witch the world fears.

19. Inheritance

She paints the girl she used to be, in brushstrokes soft and small.
The light forgives the ivory dress, that dares not fear the fall.
A bloom sits quiet on the sill; its petals hold their breath.
Some lessons live beyond the frame, and love outlasts the rest.
The room remembers every hue, each silence, shade and tone.
The art of teaching someone else, what once you learned alone.

20. Green Escape

The world spins loud, I light the flame,
the smoke curls, it calls no name,
thoughts untangle, walls recede,
a quiet riot in my head indeed.
The clocks run slow, the city hums,
while laughter blooms, where tension numbs,
I float, I fall, I drift, I grin,
A little chaos, tucked within.

21. Smoke Signals

I spark the green, the world grows wide,
the walls breathe in, the stars collide,
thoughts unravel, neat lines bend,
the hours drift, No rush, No end.
A laugh erupts, a sigh escapes
Reality folds in smoky shapes,
I ride the haze, I float, I spin,
A tiny war, a gentle sin.

22. In Spite of Ourselves

I steal your hoodie, you steal my fries,
We've been laughing at life
and each other for a thousand tries.
You roll your eyes, I grin too wide,
We've survived the storms,
and still we collide.
In spite of ourselves, in spite of the years,
We still fight, we still love,
we still cheer through the tears.
You're my chaos, my calm, my fire and muse,
In spite of ourselves, I'll always choose you.
We dance in the kitchen with spilled coffee and crumbs,
trip over the dog, laugh till we're numb.
Every street, every night, every silly old fight,
turns into a story we hold tight.
Over a decade, still wild, still free,
I'm still yours, and you're still for me.
Through the nonsense, the love, the thrill, I'd do it all
again - and I always will.

23. Fallen Star

You burned in shadows, black and cold,
A throne of hate you claim.
The light we shared, now distant, sold,
A spark I cannot name.
I reach through fire, endless night,
but hands can grasp no ghost.
Your voice, a blade, still haunts my fight,
the one I loved the most.
The galaxy reels beneath our pain,
balance trembling thin.
I stand alone in sun and rain,
A war both lost and kin.
Yet in the void, a whisper stays,
A hope too small, too slight.
That even dark devours its prey, and bends at last to light.

24. Breakfast in the Morning

The sun begins his gentle route
across my humble floor
I take my coffee with regret
and yesterday once more.
He lingers in the buttered crumb,
the silence wears his name.
I taste the lessons softly burnt,
yet love remains the same.
A sparrow interrupts my thought,
Reminds me life resumes
That morning is a second chance
And hope has many rooms.

25. Cosmic Witch

I borrowed Saturn's rings for a bracelet,
Sprinkled moon dust in the mayors face yet.
I ride comets, yell at Mars, Store black holes in lidded jars,
Stars bend when I cough too loud,
Nebulas giggle; planets bow proud.
I'm the chaos the universe forgot,
A Witch on the loose and I like it hot!

26. Tangled Lace

I slide the lace, it bites just right,
a spark, a tease, a little bite.
Fingers trace what words can't touch,
A laugh, a smirk, and just enough. Delicate? Maybe.
Dangerous? True.
I wear this lace, all for you.

27. For the One Who Keeps Me Wild

I steal your hoodies, eat your snacks,
Tease your lips, then lean to relax.
Whisper my chaos, feel the touch,
You know me wild, know me much.

28. Unlined

I counted dots that missed the line
and found a rose in red,
where structure faltered - soft, alive.
The orange swelled like wings
that brushed the air too quick to catch
and I held my breath to hear the universal sound.
Lost and found,
both at once the canvas asked my hands
to move and whispered
secrets I almost knew.
Creation is a quiet burn
that bends the edges of my day
and leaves a mark I cannot turn
or sweep too quickly away.
The dots that missed their perfect pace
become a rose I cannot chase
and wings of orange trace the air
Reminding me that life is rare.

29. Citrus Skin

I split the orange open
It bled light.
My hands smelled like morning,
but my thoughts were last night's fire.

30. Alchemy

An orange on the counter,
Soft with waiting.
I could eat it or forgive myself.
Either way, something sweet will end.

31. The Softest Sin

I bit the berry
it bit back.
Sweet turned iron,
love turned lack.

32. When the Empire Fell

The streets were teeth - broken,
gnashing through the rust of yesterday.
Even the statues bled rust,
their marble eyes turned inward,
blind to the ash collecting in their mouths.
We built our dreams from bone and oil,
smeared our reflections on glass towers,
Called it progress, Called it God.
But God was a mirror, and we cracked him.
Now the flags hang like tired tongues,
the anthems choke on smoke,
and the gold peels off the ceilings,
like old skin.
Still, I stand, ankle-deep in the empires shadow,
and whisper its name, just to hear it die again.

33. We See You

We see the towers you build,
the speeches you polish,
the promises you tuck into pockets
while Streets crumble beneath our feet.
Satellites hum above
Catching your lies, your negligence tracking
the hunger you turn away.
Do you think we do not notice
the empty cupboards, the frozen streets.
The children waiting for someone
to remember Their names?
We are not quiet.
We are the weight of the streets.
The pulse of the people you leave behind.
We are fire and we rise above your towers.
We are the pulse,
You cannot mute.
The storm you cannot hide from.
And the sky itself carries the reckoning
You refuse to feel.

When we ignite your apathy will burn in the light we have become.

34. Hollow

Children sit in shadows,
their mouths open, empty as the sky.
We walk by— pretending "fullness heals."

35. Gnaw

The bread is gone— and so is everything else.
Hands reach but touch only air.
I taste hunger in my own veins.

36. Quiet Riot

Their eyes are factories of silent protest.
We give coins they need worlds.
I hear the hunger whisper my name.

37. Haze of Whispers

They live in the corners,
Where dust remembers breath.
I don't see them, but my name bends in the air,
like a candle about to die.

38. Mirror Light

A ghost brushed my cheek,
it felt like recognition.
Maybe I'm the haunting,
and this body is what's left behind.

39. Closer to the Edge

I've been counting every dollar like it's sacred,
Stretching dreams between the rent and the sky.
There's a crack in every promise they painted,
And the headlines tell me who to despise.
But my neighbor shared her garden's tomatoes, Said, "We rise by keeping each other alive."
So we plant what's left of our tomorrows, In the dirt where our hope can survive.
We're tired of begging kings for mercy, When the throne is built out of greed.
There's still beauty we can't let fade away.
So I'll trade my fear for something human, and my silence for a seed.
If the sky falls down, we'll lift it together,
We've been broken, but we're built for the pressure.
We're Closer to the edge than the crown, But we'll keep reaching up, we won't drown.
They can't buy the soul of forever,
If the sky falls down, we'll lift it together.
There's a billboard selling heaven for credit, But the air

outside's too thick to breathe.
Kids draw oceans they've never visited, In schools that leak when it rains in the spring.
And I still walk past that maple tree growing
Through the cracks in the parking lot's gray
Proof the Earth keeps softly showing.
Maybe Change won't come from power,
But from hands that hold and hearts that vow
To mend the ground, to love the hours,
To start the healing here and now.
Yeah, we're Closer to the edge... Than we are to the crown.

40. Where I'll Lay My Scars

Someday I would like to be
Way up where the birds do sing.
Way above the clouds and stars
That is where I'll lay my scars.
I'll trade my pain for open skies,
Let the wind unmask my tired eyes,
I'd lay my baggage at the gate,
And swear to God to never be late.
No weight of past, no heavy chain,
Just morning dew instead of rain,
Up there I'll breathe, at last, free
There's nowhere else I'd rather be.
The world below can spin and fade,
I'll rest where peace and dreams are made.

41. The Price of Bread

We barter peace for paper bills,
and smile through shallow breath.
The wealthy dine on daffodils,
The rest make meals of death.
Our dreams are taxed, our hearts are sold,
for crowns we'll never wear.
While silence screams in bars of gold,
And mercy costs a prayer.
The sun still shines - though rationed now,
Behind a billboards face.
We learn to bow, forget the how, and call it "Saving Grace."
Yet somewhere in the Ash and gray,
A child recalls the sky.
And whispers softly to the day, that hope refused to die.

42. Capitalist Hunger

We sell our time, we sell our sweat,
The towers rise while we forget,
Presidents smile with teeth of gold,
The districts starve, the market's sold.
Screens blink our worth, our choices bought,
Every rebellion silently caught,
We bow, we buy, we choke, we plead,
While profit feasts on human need.

43. Paycheck Ghost

We bleed our hours, they sip their wine,
Our paychecks whisper "you are fine."
The bosses grin, their pockets burst,
We scrape and scrape, our hunger cursed.
The rent devours, the fridge is bare,
Our labor cheap, their yachts declare,
We buy, we cry, we beg, we steal,
While capitalism signs the deal.

44. Good Boy Forbin

They say one day this will get easier,
But I think they lie.
The silence where your paws should be,
Is only where I cry.
My good boy Forbin ran so fast,
to meet the suns first ray,
And though I miss your gentle bark,
you walk with me each day.

45. On the Cross

Are you running away or running toward it
Fate was a blade yeah you can't ignore it
You sold the truth for a hit of control
Spit on the wound and called it your soul

The void still calls it's sweet and loud
Breaking hearts still drawing crowds
Don't you dare give in this time
We're all just sinners in a line

Why give up why go on
The greatest yet is dead and gone
All of this can't be undone
I'm fucking done

On the cross not for your god
Hanging for the pain that built this façade.

They're bringing guns while we starve at home
Screaming through screens still die alone

On the cross not to repent
Just to carry the weight they never meant

Start it up press rewind
Somewhere way back in time
Some white men drew the crown
And now we all drown

Blood on the streets no peace no stop
Sirens sing while the bodies drop
Shots in the dark echo through town
The world is scary it's burning down

Feed the rich ignore the poor
Pray for peace but fund the war
Saints in suits still call it sin
While they sell the air we're breathing in

On the cross not for your god
Hanging for the pain that built this façade
They're bringing guns while we starve at home
Screaming through screens still die alone

On the cross not to repent
Just to carry the weight they never meant

We bleed for bills we beg for light

We drown in day we choke at night
They said be still we said we tried
Now all that's left are those who lied

Start it up rewind the cost
We all hang here on the cross
Not for heaven not for grace
Just to look our pain in the face

46. I am the Signal

I was waiting for the universe to blink
Counting stars just to see what they'd think
Every red light, every turn I missed
I thought fate was hidden in the mist

But maybe it was me all along
Caught between the static and the song
I'm done chasing after signs in the sky
No more asking reasons why

I'm the current, I'm the sound
I'm the pulse that moves the ground
I don't need a map, don't need permission

stopped searching
I became the signal

I used to pray to headlights on the road
Hoping they'd tell me where to go
But every time the silence spoke

I felt the frequency in my bones

Now I'm tuned to something real
The only truth I need to feel
I'm done chasing after signs in the sky
No more asking reasons why

I'm the current, I'm the sound
I'm the pulse that moves the ground
I don't need a map, don't need permission
I stopped searching
I became the signal

Static fades, the noise falls out
My heart transmits, I'm breaking out
No waiting, no more please just show
I'm green light baby time to go

I'm done chasing after signs in the sky
No more asking reasons why
I'm the hum beneath the city's glow
Every heartbeat says I know

I don't need a map, don't need permission
I stopped searching
I became the signal

47. Mirrorball Mind

Round, spinning, spinning,
I see my face in fragments
Every smile is someone else
Every eye in the crowd is empty

I am reflection chasing reflection
A disco of thoughts
I try to hold one, it shatters
Light hits my skin

I sparkle

I ache

I sparkle more

Nobody notices.

48. Falling Deeper

Falling falling
Rabbit hole rabbit hole
Keys keys keys keys
Stained glass skies, crack my eyes

Time melts, I synthesize
Flowers scream in neon hue
Smoke curls, I breathe in you
Key in my hand, it bites, it hums

Doors open up, the rabbit comes
Falling falling deeper down
Lost my mind, but found the crown
Falling down falling down rabbit hole

Glass garden blooms, I lose control
Keys in my pocket, doors in my head
I keep falling deeper instead
Falling down falling down rabbit hole

Glass garden blooms, I lose control
Time explodes, mind untied
Weed in my lungs, nowhere to hide
Mirrors whisper, I answer slow

Shadows dance in a toxic glow
Clock ticks backward, petals collide
Edge of the world is where I hide
Key in my hand, it bites, it hums

Doors open up, the rabbit comes
Falling falling deeper down
Lost my mind, but found the crown
Falling down falling down rabbit hole

Glass garden blooms, I lose control
Keys in my pocket, doors in my head
I keep falling deeper instead
Falling down falling down rabbit hole

Glass garden blooms, I lose control
Time explodes, mind untied
Weed in my lungs, nowhere to hide
Neon rain, synthetic flowers

Electric hearts, collapsing hours
Stained glass eyes, glitch in my soul

I am lost, I am gold, I am control
Falling down falling down rabbit hole

Glass garden blooms, I lose control
Keys in my pocket, doors in my head
I keep falling deeper instead
Falling down falling down rabbit hole

Glass garden blooms, I lose control
Time explodes, mind untied
Weed in my lungs, nowhere to hide.

Rabbit rabbit rabbit hole

Keys keys keys

Falling falling

49. Footing the Bill

They smile with gold in their teeth,
While I count coins for heat.
The wires hum like hymns of greed,
And I still pay to breathe.

They raise the rates, we bite our tongues,
They toast their yachts, we scrape the crumbs.
Our sweat, their dividends,
Our cries, their violins.

We built the grid they stand upon,
And somehow we're the ones who're wrong.
Why are we footing the bill?!
While their pockets overflow and still—

We bleed just to stay alive,
They drain the light from our eyes!
Health ain't a luxury, it's life—
But they sell it for a price!

We the people, we the ghosts,
Carrying a country that forgot its oath!
Dental, vision, dreams deferred,
Insurance plans are empty words.

A home should be a human right,
Not a number lost to corporate might.
They paved the streets with promises,
And billed us for the lies.

They privatized our hope,
Then blamed us when it died.
Oh say, can you see—
The bodies under your money trees?

We're drowning in electric seas,
While you toast "efficiency."
Your profits are our poverty,
Your "growth" our broken knees.

Why are we footing the bill?!
For your towers and your pills?!
You call it freedom, call it fair—
But the middle class is gasping air!

You've sold our souls for subsidies,
Dressed in false democracies!

We the people—
We remember.
And we are coming for what's ours.

There's a reckoning in the wires,
A whisper through the static fire.
We are the current you can't kill—
And we're done footing your bill.

50. Insurance Copays and Golden Ladders

Insurance copays and golden ladders
Can't buy back the health that time has shattered.
Empty pockets jingling with regret,
While the rich get richer off our sweat.

The gap keeps widening. It's plain to see.
The rich get richer, but you and me.
We work our fingers to the bone,
But the 'American dream' feels so far gone.

The system's rigged, the rich get richer,
While the poor man struggles, getting sicker.
Empty pockets jingling with regret,
While the precious moments tick, tick, tick.

Time is slipping, and were all feeling the cost.
As dreams are dying, all hope cant be lost.

The gap keeps widening. It's plain to see.

The rich get richer, but you and me.
We work our fingers to the bone,
But the 'American dream' feels so far gone.

Sickness and disease, they don't discriminate.
Yet the scales of healing tip with fate.
The rich get healed, while the poor just wait.

Imagine a place where care's a right, not a struggle or fight.
Universal healthcare, a beacon of fairness, shining bright.
Preventive measures, early detection.
A society focused on well-being's direction
We need a cure for inequality and its unyielding projection.

www.ingramcontent.com/pod-product-compliance
Lightning Source LLC
Chambersburg PA
CBHW060352050426
42449CB00011B/2949